IT'S THE END OF THE WORLD!

GLOBAL PANDEMIC

BY ALLAN MOREY

BELLWETHER MEDIA • MINNEAPOLIS, MN

™

Are you ready to take it to the extreme? Torque books thrust you into the action-packed world of sports, vehicles, mystery, and adventure. These books may include dirt, smoke, fire, and chilling tales. WARNING: read at your own risk.

This edition first published in 2020 by Bellwether Media, Inc.

Library of Congress Cataloging-in-Publication Data

Names: Morey, Allan, author.
Title: Global Pandemic / by Allan Morey.
Description: Minneapolis, MN : Bellwether Media, Inc., [2020] |
   Series: Torque: It's the End of the World! | Audience: Ages 7-12. |
   Audience: Grades 3 to 7. | Includes bibliographical references and index.
Identifiers: LCCN 2019000941 (print) | LCCN 2019002136 (ebook) | ISBN
   9781618916525 (ebook) | ISBN 9781644870815 (hardcover : alk. puper)
Subjects: LCSH: Epidemics–Juvenile literature. | Communicable diseases-
   Juvenile literature.
Classification: LCC RA653.5 (ebook) | LCC RA653.5 .M67 2020 (print) |
   DDC 614–dc23
LC record available at https://lccn.loc.gov/2019000941

Editor: Rebecca Sabelko   Designer: Andrea Schneider

Printed in the United States of America, North Mankato, MN.

TABLE OF CONTENTS

You are on your way home from a trip overseas. You saw **native** animals. You tried new food. The trip was a blast!

You try to get comfortable for your flight home. But someone behind you keeps coughing. The person is shaking and has a fever. You wonder if the person is seriously ill. You also worry that others might get sick.

Soon the plane lands. Everyone is told to stay in their seats. A medical team wearing gloves and masks boards the plane. They lead the sick person away.

You learn there is a deadly flu **outbreak**. It started in the country you visited. If it spreads, there could be a global pandemic!

TOO FAST TO BE STOPPED

A pandemic is a widespread outbreak of an **infectious** disease. The disease might be a new **virus**. It could also be a **bacterial** infection.

A pandemic starts in a populated place. The disease travels quickly from person to person. It moves too fast to be stopped!

There are four types of disease. They include infectious diseases as well as diseases that you get when your body is missing something it needs. Some people are born with a disease. Other diseases happen because body parts do not work properly.

Governments around the world try to stop a pandemic from happening. They alert other countries of outbreaks. They stop travel. But these warnings do not always work!

Thousands of people become ill! They are not able to work. Businesses close, and factories shut down. Hospitals run out of medicine and supplies. Society begins to shut down. People panic as they run out of food.

CHAIN REACTION

a disease begins in a populated area

infected people travel and infect more people around the world

businesses shut down and hospitals run out of supplies

people run out of food

HOW ARE POSSIBLE?

Pandemics can happen in several ways. A new disease may appear that people are not **immune** to. Two viruses can come together to create a new and deadly virus. A disease that affects animals can also change. It might start making people ill, too.

BOOK TITLE: **FEVER 1793**

AUTHOR:
LAURIE HALSE ANDERSON

YEAR RELEASED: **2000**

About the book: **A deadly fever spreads throughout Philadelphia in the summer of 1793. The sickness reaches Mattie's family. Her mother pushes her to leave the city with her grandfather. They soon find the fever is everywhere. They must find a way to survive.**

Could it happen?: **Diseases have the ability to spread quickly. It is possible for an entire community to become ill in a short amount of time.**

! SWINE FLU

The swine flu affects pigs' ability to breathe. There are cases of this disease spreading to people.

Diseases are always looking for a **host**. A bubonic plague happened in the middle of the 1300s. Some people believe it started with infected fleas and lice that attached themselves to human hosts. Then the disease spread from person to person through coughing.

ILLUSTRATION OF LICE ON HUMAN SKIN

Cholera is a bacterial disease that affects the intestines. People become ill when they drink or eat something infected with the bacteria.

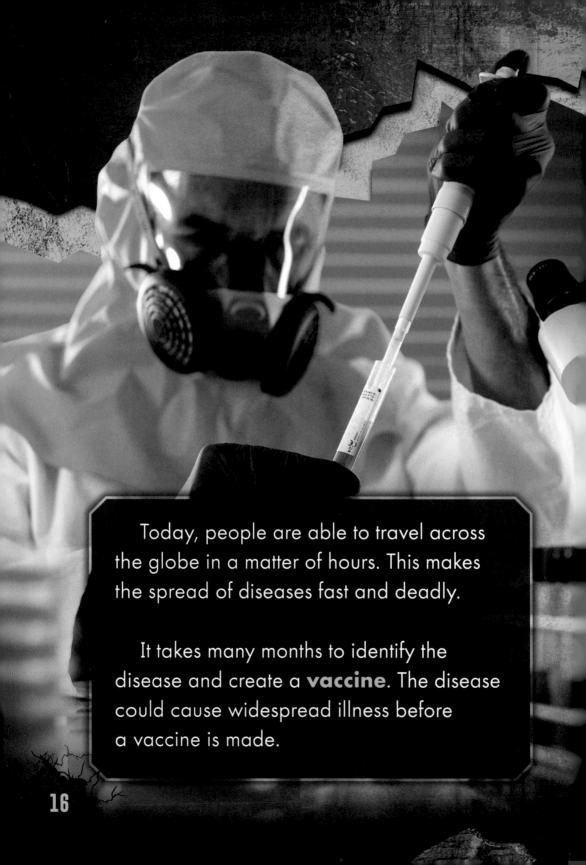

Today, people are able to travel across the globe in a matter of hours. This makes the spread of diseases fast and deadly.

It takes many months to identify the disease and create a **vaccine**. The disease could cause widespread illness before a vaccine is made.

A LOOK BACK: THE BUBONIC PLAGUES

JUSTINIAN PLAGUE

MID-500s
- more than 25 million people died
- spread throughout the Roman Empire

BACTERIA THAT CAUSED THE BUBONIC PLAGUES

THE BLACK DEATH

MID-1300s
- more than half the people living in Europe died
- spread from Asia to Europe

MODERN PLAGUE

MID-1800s
- nearly 10 million people died
- spread throughout Asia

HOW LIKELY  IS A GLOBAL PANDEMIC?

Global pandemics have happened in the past. It is likely that one will happen again.

Scientists hope to stop pandemics by spotting new diseases. They study how new diseases spread. They learn what **symptoms** the diseases cause. This helps scientists take steps to stop the spread of new diseases.

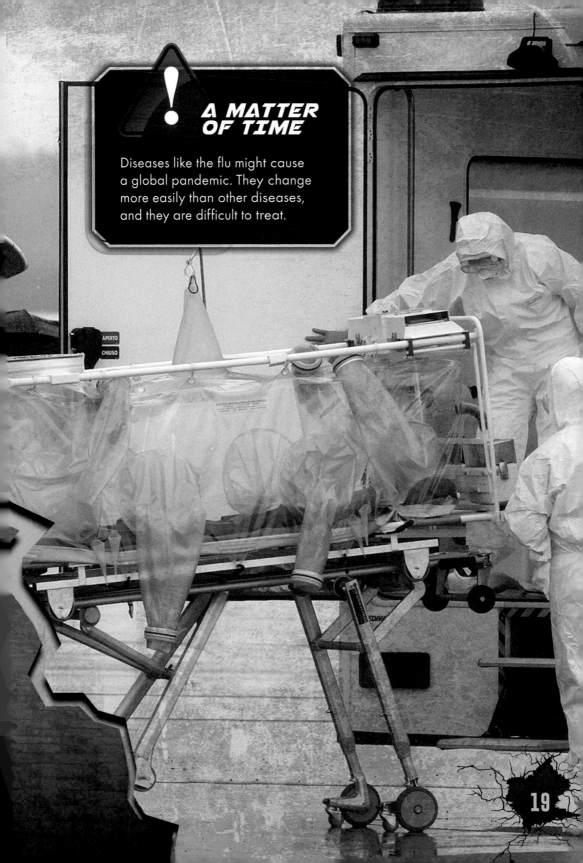

A MATTER OF TIME

Diseases like the flu might cause a global pandemic. They change more easily than other diseases, and they are difficult to treat.

SPANISH FLU

There was a global flu pandemic in 1918. It was called the Spanish flu. It spread to parts of North America, Europe, and Asia. An estimated 50 million people died!

There are ways you can fight a pandemic. Stay home if you are sick. Cover your mouth and nose when you cough. If you are healthy, wash your hands often, and avoid contact with sick people. These actions keep germs from spreading. Practicing healthy habits can keep people safe during an outbreak!

GLOSSARY

bacterial—having to do with singled-celled living things called bacteria; bacteria usually live in soil, water, or in plants and animals.

host—a living animal or plant that a disease or parasite lives on or in; a parasite is a living thing, such as a flea, that takes its food and shelter from other living things without giving back.

immune—not capable of being infected by a disease

infectious—capable of spreading, such as a disease going from one person to another

native—a kind of plant or animal that originally grew or lived in a particular place

outbreak—the sudden spread of a disease

symptoms—signs of a disease

vaccine—a medicine created to keep people from being infected by diseases

virus—something that causes a disease

TO LEARN MORE

AT THE LIBRARY

Denton, Michelle. *Pandemics: Deadly Disease Outbreaks.*
New York, N.Y.: Lucent Press, 2020.

Griffin, Mary. *The Black Death.* New York, N.Y.: Gareth
Stevens Publishing, 2020.

Krasner, Barbara. *Influenza: How the Flu Changed History.*
North Mankato, Minn.: Capstone Press, 2019.

ON THE WEB

FACTSURFER

Factsurfer.com gives you
a safe, fun way to find
more information.
1. Go to www.factsurfer.com
2. Enter "global pandemic" into the search box
   and click Q.
3. Select your book cover to see a list
   of related web sites.

INDEX